Dr. Hollis Lynch, Professor of History and Director of the Institute of African Studies at Columbia University, is the consultant for the Toward Freedom books. He brings to this program experience as a teacher, author, and editor of West African and Afro-American subjects. A native of Trinidad, Dr. Lynch's lifelong involvement in black history includes an active membership in the Association for the Study of Negro Life and History and the African Studies Association.

Saddles and Sabers

BLACK MEN IN THE OLD WEST

by LaVere Anderson

illustrated by Herman Vestal

Toward Freedom Series

GARRARD PUBLISHING COMPANY CHAMPAIGN, ILLINOIS

To Daniel French Thixton

Library of Congress Cataloging in Publication Data

Anderson, LaVere.
  Saddles and sabers, Black men in the old west

  (Toward freedom series)
  SUMMARY: Brief biographies of black cowboys, lawmen,
and cavalry soldiers who helped settle the West during
the latter half of the nineteenth century.

  1. Negroes—Biography—Juvenile literature.
2. Negroes—The West—Juvenile literature. 3. The
West—Biography—Juvenile literature. [1. Negroes—
Biography. 2. The West—Biography] I. Vestal,
Herman B., illus. II. Title. III. Series.
E185.925.A65   917.8′06′96073 [B] [920]   74–18122
ISBN 0–8116–4805–2

Picture credits:

The Bettmann Archive: p. 41
Jose Cisneros, courtesy of John M. Carroll: p. 120
Culver Pictures: pp. 17, 61
Denver Public Library, Western History Department: pp. 81,
    84 (bottom), 100
Library of Congress, Erwin E. Smith Collection: p. 97
New York Public Library, Picture Collecton: pp. 6, 84 (top)
University of Oklahoma Library, Western History Collections: pp. 67,
    70, 107, 110

81-569   (1984-85)

Contents

They Helped Build the West

The Old West was a very special place and time. It stretched beyond the Mississippi River to the Pacific Ocean and from Canada to Mexico. It lasted fifty years, from about 1850 to 1900. In that place and time the nation completed its westward expansion, and the vast territory with its riches of furs, gold, and fertile soil became a new home to great numbers of Americans. Among them were many thousands of black men.

The activities of those black men in the West are poorly recorded. We know little about such a man as Isaiah Dorman, only what could be pieced together years later from the memories of his friends and the reports of Indians who fought in the battle where he died. However, there are a few men of whom we know much. Nat Love is one. He wrote the story of his life and became the only black cowboy of his time to write an autobiography.

The stories in this book are of cowboys, lawmen, and cavalry soldiers. They were the men in the saddles.

There are enough clues and parts of stories to tell us that black westerners were active in many other kinds of frontier work. Some were farmers. Some were trappers. Some laid railroad tracks across the broad plains, or set telegraph poles. Some were gold miners. Infantry—foot soldiers—stood guard at water holes, walked beside slow-moving wagon trains, fought forest fires.

They all helped to build the West and reshape our nation. Their skill and energy and blood went into the struggle. Their stories are a part of the heritage of America.

1. Nat Love: "Deadwood Dick"

The small boy stared at the big black horse. The horse was Highwayman. He had never been ridden, and there was a wicked gleam in his eyes. The boy was Nat Love, born a slave in a log cabin near Nashville, Tennessee. He'd been seven years old when the Civil War began. Now the war was over, the slaves were free, and Nat was twelve. He was undersized for his age, but he was a wiry boy.

To help support his mother, Nat worked on the big Williams Horse Ranch a few miles from his home. He earned his money by breaking colts—taming them so they could be ridden.

The young horses did not like to be broken. They ran, jumped, kicked, and tossed. Even mounting such a colt was a problem. He had to be backed into a stall and held until the rider could get a firm seat on his back. Then somebody opened the stall gate, and out into the corral the colt went like a shot.

Rancher Williams's corral had seen some fiery young animals, but Nat stuck to their bare backs like molasses to a biscuit. When he had ridden a bucking colt until it could buck no more, the colt was considered broken and Nat collected ten cents for his work. Then he wiped his sweating face, drove a fresh colt into a stall, and managed to get onto its back. He stayed there until he had earned another dime.

Rancher Williams had two sons about Nat's age. On a summer day in 1866, when their father was away, they challenged Nat. "Bet you can't ride Highwayman," one said.

"Bet I can," Nat answered. "For fifty cents."

"Bet you can't. For twenty-five cents."

Nat took a hard look at the big rough horse. Highwayman was no colt. And he was guaranteed mean. But twenty-five cents was a lot of money.

"Bet I can," Nat said, "for twenty-five cents paid in advance."

The boys paid him. Nat tied the money into a corner of his shirttail for safekeeping.

It took the efforts of all three boys to get the horse into a stall. As soon as Nat scrambled on his back, Highwayman began to jump. The Williams boys opened the stall gate and sprang aside. Out into the corral shot the furious horse in a leap that almost toppled Nat.

Around the corral Highwayman plunged. Then he jumped the rail fence and galloped off across the green fields. Nat yelled. The Williams boys shouted. Every dog within hearing began to bark and run after the horse. Highwayman galloped across an open pasture where mares grazed with their colts. Mothers and babies promptly joined the race.

The noisy parade attracted the attention of some ranchers. "It looks like a runaway!" they said.

Hurriedly they mounted their horses and started in pursuit, but nobody could catch Highwayman. Nat, all hunched up like a toad, clung to the horse's mane. He couldn't stop the horse and he couldn't get off without falling off and perhaps breaking his neck.

Highwayman easily outran his followers. He covered miles. He jumped fences as if they were anthills. His black hide glistened with sweat, and his breath came hard. At last he began to tire. His pace slowed. He came to another fence, but he had no heart to jump it. He stopped.

Cautiously Nat sat up. He smiled with relief and stroked the horse's steaming shoulder. "Good boy," he said. "Good old Highwayman."

Still smiling, Nat patted the corner of his shirt-tail where he'd tied his twenty-five cents. Suddenly his smile faded. The knot had come untied during the wild ride. The money was gone.

"You're the best rider in Tennessee!" the Williams boys shouted when Nat rode into the corral on his well-broken mount.

"Thanks," said Nat unhappily, thinking that he never wanted to see a horse again. Yet soon he was breaking another colt. He kept his job for three years.

Then one day a man named Johnson said he would raffle a fine horse for fifty cents a chance. Nat wanted to buy a chance on that horse, but he had no money.

He did have a few chickens. The money he made by selling their eggs was a big part of his income. Should he risk some of the chickens on a raffle? It would be taking a dreadful chance. Still, he might win.

He caught two of the biggest hens and sold them for fifty cents. He bought a raffle ticket. And this time Nat Love didn't lose his money. He won the horse.

When Mr. Johnson offered to buy the horse back for fifty dollars, Nat sold. The boy had never seen so much money before, but he knew how he wanted to use it. He had heard that there were large cattle ranches in the western part of the United States where good horsemen were needed to handle the herds.

"I'm good with horses," he thought. "If I go out there I can get a real job with real pay."

He told his mother, "Mama, here is half of my money. It should last until I can send you some more. I'm going out West and get a ranch job."

Quick tears came to his mother's eyes, but she nodded her head. "It will be hard to see you go, son, but I'll not try to stop you," she said. "There are too many poor black boys in Tennessee and hardly any work for them. You'll have a better chance to make something of yourself out West."

On a February morning in 1869, fifteen-year-old Nat Love left Tennessee. Over his shoulder he carried a cloth sack. It held some cornbread and bacon and an extra pair of socks.

It is a long way from Tennessee to the West, and it is a cold way in February. Nat tramped down icy roads and across frozen fields. Sometimes he got a ride on a farm wagon. Sometimes, in return for some wood-chopping, a farmer's wife gave him a hot meal. Spring had come before he reached a little frontier town in Kansas where cattle from western ranches were shipped by railroad to markets in the East.

When Nat arrived in town he found the streets alive with cowpunchers. He watched in amazement as the punchers, whooping and firing their guns, galloped by on their tough range ponies. He soon learned that these men had just collected their pay for driving a herd of longhorn cattle up from Texas, and they were in a mood to celebrate. And he saw that there were some black cowboys among them.

"I'm not the first man born in a slave cabin to get the idea of coming West," he thought.

Next morning Nat went to the herders' camp outside of town and asked the camp boss if he needed any help.

"Can you ride a wild horse?" the boss asked.

"Yes, sir."

The boss turned to a cowboy. "Bronco Jim, go out and rope old Good Eye. We'll see if this fellow can ride."

As Bronco Jim saddled Good Eye, he whispered to Nat, "Watch out for this critter. He's a bad one— mean as they come."

Confidently, Nat swung onto the horse while the grinning Texans watched. Whee! Years later Nat would tell how Good Eye was the worst horse he had ever ridden. But as with Highwayman, Nat rode because he couldn't get off without falling off. And how the Texans cheered! They had been ready to make a fool of Nat when they thought he was a tenderfoot, but they had respect for a good rider.

"I'll pay you thirty dollars a month," the surprised camp boss told Nat when the ride was over. "We leave at sunup tomorrow for the Red River and home. What's your name?"

"Nat Love."

"We've already got a Nat in this outfit. We'll call you Dick." The boss paused. "That's hardly enough name. Let's make it Red River Dick."

So Nat Love of Tennessee became Red River Dick of Texas.

They gave him a horse, a saddle, a bridle, and spurs. They gave him tough leather chaps to wear over his patched trousers, boots, a pair of warm blankets, and a .45 Colt revolver. Proudly Nat put on his new outfit and paraded around camp. He wished that his mother could see him now.

At sunrise next morning the Duval outfit rode south toward Texas. They were fourteen men and Nat. They had been on the trail only a day when a large band of well-armed Indians came shouting out of a patch of timber to attack them. In the first moments of fighting a cowboy near Nat was killed.

Nat thought for sure his time had come to die. He was too frightened even to run away.

"Use your gun!" Bronco Jim yelled at him.

Nat got out his new Colt. He had never fired a gun in his life, but now he shot fast.

The fight was short and sharp. The Indian warriors were after the men's extra saddle horses and their packs of food and gear. They got the saddle horses by stampeding the herd, and they snatched the pack horses in a blaze of gunfire. Satisfied, they rode away leaving thirteen cowboys and Nat to bury a dead comrade and start the long walk to Texas. With only six horses left among fourteen riders, it was a slow trip. Summer had almost come to the prairies before Nat at last saw his new home, a fine ranch in the western Panhandle in Texas.

A cowboy's life—Nat Love in Tennessee could never have imagined what the real thing was like. But Red River Dick took to "cowboying" as though he had been born on the range.

Nat soon felt a genuine love for the wild free life of the plains and for the cowboys who were his comrades. He thought a braver, truer set of men never lived. They were always ready to share their blankets or their last bit of food with a needy companion. When trouble struck—and it struck often—many a cowboy risked his life to save another.

The work on a cattle ranch was hard. Nat learned to rope and brand wild cattle, and to spend long hours in the saddle driving the slow herds up the dusty cow trails to northern markets. He learned to brave lightning and hailstorms and stampedes, to fight off outlaws and Indians.

He learned that there was little law in the great

Deadwood Dick "took to cowboying as though he had been born on the range." He is seen here, with saddle and rifle, ready for any adventure that might present itself.

lonely stretches of the West and that a man's life might depend on how fast and straight he could shoot a gun. So Nat practiced with his .45 Colt every chance he got. At first, about all he could hit was a barn door, if the door wasn't too far away. In time he could shoot better than any other man on the ranch.

After three years in Texas, Nat moved to Arizona to work for a larger outfit. For years he rode the ranges and covered all the trails south to Mexico and north to the Dakotas.

He learned to speak Spanish and to read and write. He became known as a "top hand" and the hero of many a fight on the trail. Nat had been wise to go West and to learn a trade well in a land where good men were scarce. Ex-slaves who stayed in the South often were treated almost as badly as slaves, but on western ranches a man was respected for the job he could do. Blacks and whites worked together and shared the same dangers and the same campfires.

Often on a dark night Nat and his comrades sat around a campfire telling stories about their experiences. Nat could tell some wonderful yarns.

"We were pushing 500 head of longhorns up the trail to Wyoming," he would begin softly. "One midnight we heard a roaring noise in the north. It sounded like thunder, but we knew it was a buffalo stampede.

"We all went out with our guns. We thought if

we killed enough of the front buffalo, the rest would change course and not go through our herd of cattle. Well, we shot and shot, but those buffalo paid no more attention to us than they would have to little boys with pea shooters.

"One of our young fellows, Cal Surcy, was having trouble with his mount. Before any of us could reach him, his horse bolted right in front of those buffalo. The whole stampede ran over them. All we could ever find later of poor Cal were a few scraps of his clothes, and what was left of his horse looked about the size of a jackrabbit.

"The buffalo went straight through our herd. In the dark we couldn't see how much damage they'd done, but when dawn came we found a lot of our cattle lying dead or crippled in the dust, and the rest were scattered all over the plains.

"It took our outfit two days to round them up for the trail again."

Or Nat might tell about the time he was captured by Indians in Yellow Horse Canyon, after a running fight in which he was badly wounded. "The Indians spared my life," he would say, "because I'd killed five of them in the fight and proved myself a brave man. Bravery counts with Indians, you know." The Indians dressed his wounds with a salve made from herbs, and the wounds healed quickly.

"That was good salve all right," Nat said. "But when they wanted me to marry the chief's daughter and be a member of the tribe—they named me Buffalo Papoose!—I stole a pony and escaped one cloudy night. I rode for twelve hours and didn't stop riding until I was safe on the home ranch again."

Nat had dozens of stories to tell about his feats. Probably he exaggerated some of the stories a little, for he liked to show off. Most cowboys liked to show off a bit. But if anyone doubted that Nat was a great all-around cowboy, they lost those doubts on July 4, 1876, in Deadwood City in the Dakota Territory.

That spring Nat's Arizona outfit had an order for 3,000 head of steers to be delivered near Deadwood. It was a large order, but they filled it and arrived in Dakota on July third with their herd in good shape.

Deadwood at holiday time was a lively place. Every puncher from miles around had come to town to celebrate the Fourth.

Some of the gamblers and mining men made up a purse of $200 for a roping contest. Twelve mustangs —the most vicious dozen of the lot—were cut from a herd of wild horses just off the range. The idea was that the dozen competing cowboys were each to rope, throw, tie, bridle, saddle, and mount a particular mustang in the shortest possible time. The fastest time would win.

When all was ready, the starting gun cracked. Out sprang the twelve cowboys together, each making for his mount. Nat's trail boss had picked the mustangs, and the one Nat got was the worst of the bunch. The horse had no name, but before Nat could rope and tie it, he had his own name for the animal—Red Hot Mustard!

When Nat finally mounted the furious horse, there was nothing to be seen for a moment but dust and hoofs. The mustang bucked and kicked. It reared on its hind legs. It doubled up like a jackknife. It did everything but lie down and roll over on its rider. All the while a whooping Nat kept "sticking in" with his spurs, and using his quirt on the horse's flanks. Riding the mustang was not part of the contest, but Nat was having fun.

His time in mounting had been exactly 9 minutes. The next best time was 12½ minutes. That gave Nat the purse.

But the Fourth was not over for Deadwood. Next came a shooting contest with rifle and .45 Colt.

The range was measured off—100 and 250 yards for the rifle, a shorter distance for the Colt. Then the bull's-eyes went up. To Nat they looked about the size of apples—small apples.

A puncher named Stormy Jim was competing, and he was said to be the best shot in the West. Jim put eight of his fourteen rifle shots into the bull's-eye, and five of his revolver shots. That was good shooting. But this was Nat's day. Nat put every one of his fourteen rifle shots in the bull's-eye with ease. Ten of his revolver shots went into the eye, and the others were close.

Nat had won again, and Deadwood went wild.

"Red River Dick! The Champion!" a boy shouted.

Then a man's louder voice yelled, *"Deadwood Dick! Champion Deadwood Dick!"*

The crowd took it up. Soon everybody was chanting, "Deadwood Dick!"

And was he proud—Nat Love, the boy from Tennessee!

Years later, as an old man telling how he became Deadwood Dick, Nat would say, "I have always carried the name with honor since that time."

Slowly, life changed on the prairies. Railroad tracks were laid across the rangeland, and the Iron Horse chugged its way where cowponies had once galloped. With trains whisking Texas beef straight from ranch to market, there was no longer need for cattle drives up the old trails. The best and most exciting part of cowboying was over.

So in 1890 Nat Love went back to Tennessee to see his mother. Then he left home again to look for a new career. Strangely, he found work with the railroads.

He got a job as a Pullman porter, about the only kind of well-paying job then open to blacks. Soon he was riding a train across the country he had once ridden as a cowboy.

He was happy in his new work, but sometimes as he looked out of the train windows, memories of the old life came thronging back to him. Finally he decided to write about it.

The book, published in 1907, was titled: *The Life and Adventures of Nat Love—Better Known in the Cattle Country as "Deadwood Dick."* Some of it sounded as if Nat were still "showing off" a bit, cowboy style. But no reader could doubt him when he said his chest swelled with pride because he was an American and had lived in the West and known the men of that frontier: "men whose minds were as broad as the plains they roamed, and whose creed was every man for himself and every friend for each other, and with each other till the end."

Those are good words about a rare breed of men. Nat Love said it well.

2. Isaiah Dorman: Custer Guide

Sometimes the trails of western black men crossed. Sometimes they just missed. Nat Love, herding those 3,000 steers on the way to that championship Fourth of July in Deadwood, did not know that he had missed Isaiah Dorman's trail by only 60 miles. Isaiah was riding at the head of a long line of blue-uniformed troopers, the all-white Seventh United States Cavalry commanded by Lt. Col. George A. Custer. Their march led through the Montana land of the Sioux Indians.

Isaiah was no cavalryman, no fighting man at all. He wore buckskins and a white straw hat, and his position at the head of the column was not a matter of honor. He was paid well to act as guide and interpreter for the Seventh, so he was supposed to ride up front where he could be useful.

Behind him rode a double line of several hundred troopers. Their guidons hung limply in the hot afternoon air, and dust spurted behind the iron-shod hoofs of their horses. A brassy sun glinted sharply on their guns, and far to the rear straggled their pack mules loaded with ammunition and other supplies of battle.

Isaiah's near-riders were two Indian scouts from tribes friendly to the white men. One was Bloody Knife, chief of the Arikara scouts. The other was Half-Yellow-Face, chief of the Crow scouts.

The scouts' business was to watch for signs of the Sioux, who were not friendly at all. Any Indians refusing to leave their hunting grounds and live on government reservations were considered "hostiles" by the United States government. The Sioux refused. They said—truthfully—that this land had been their people's home since time beyond memory. Moreover, the white men had signed a treaty guaranteeing Sioux rights to the land. The treaty said that no whites could enter without Indian permission. The treaty was to last forever.

On this afternoon of June 25, 1876, the treaty was less than eight years old, but the whites were already planning to lay railroad tracks across the land and stake out towns. Gold had been discovered, and men wanted to move in and mine it. The Indians were told to move to a reservation, live on government rations, and obey white men's laws. The Sioux objected. In the eyes of the whites that made them very hostile indeed.

Isaiah felt differently. He liked the Sioux. In earlier years he had lived in their villages and married a Sioux girl. He spoke the difficult Sioux language. That was why Colonel Custer had wanted him to come on this expedition as an interpreter.

To Isaiah Dorman this was no mission of war. He had agreed to come because he wanted to see again the Montana country he knew so well, and to renew old friendships. More important, he thought he might help to bring peace. His knowledge of Indians had often helped to stop trouble at the forts. Now, by palavering with his Sioux friends, he hoped to be helpful again.

Isaiah and the two scouts topped a ridge and looked down across a broad bright land. It was a varied land of gulches and ravines, separated by green plains twinkling with patches of sego lilies. Off to the south Isaiah could see the emerald fringe where cottonwood trees edged the banks of the Little Bighorn River, the river that Indians called Greasy Grass.

"Sioux," Bloody Knife said, and pointed toward the distance. Isaiah squinted against the sun.

"Look for worms," Bloody Knife told him. "This far away, running ponies look like crawling worms."

Isaiah squinted again, then shook his head. At

55, his eyes were no longer sharp. But he didn't need to see worms to know that the Sioux were near. He had seen the signs for three days now. All the scouts had. They had passed camping places and pony droppings and lodge trails. Many. Very many. The scouts had told Colonel Custer, and Isaiah had kept himself ready for the order to go out and palaver with the Sioux. He was puzzled, though, that the order was so long in coming.

"Too many worms," Bloody Knife told Isaiah as the pair moved ahead at a brisk trot.

"And too close," Isaiah said. It crossed his mind that the colonel had better be told quickly, or fighting might break out before there was time for palaver. He turned in his saddle and looked back to where Custer and some of his officers rode, just far enough behind to escape the front riders' dust. It was easy to spot the colonel. In his fringed buckskin suit and pale, broad-brimmed hat he made a bright spot among the drab blue uniforms of the other officers.

Yes, thought Isaiah, the colonel had better be told. He spoke of it to Bloody Knife.

The Arikara scout grunted, "No use. I've already told him the Sioux are close, enough Sioux to keep up fighting two or three days. The colonel listened to me, but then he just smiled and said, 'I guess we'll get through with them in one day.'" The scout shook his head. "No use telling him again."

Anger, and something like despair, swept over Isaiah. It was clear now why no order had come. The colonel didn't want to palaver. He wanted to fight!

Isaiah began to remember talk he had heard around Fort Abraham Lincoln, where the Seventh had been stationed. There were people who said the colonel was a glory seeker. They said he had been a hero in the Civil War because of his reckless bravery. He had even been given the temporary rank of a brevet major general. But the Civil War was long past, and he wanted new fame. They said he thought if he killed enough Indians he would be famous all over again, maybe famous enough to become president of the United States. Colonel Custer made no secret that he hoped someday to be President Custer. A dreadful question arose in Isaiah's mind. *Was this the day on which Custer planned to become famous again?*

If there was to be no palaver to avoid war, then why bring an interpreter? Isaiah asked himself. Suddenly he knew the answer. He was here to question Sioux survivors after the tribe had been whipped in battle.

"There's a village ahead!" Half-Yellow-Face said. He wheeled around and galloped back to Custer.

Moments later, a command to halt came down the line. Isaiah turned his horse and rode back. He found that the colonel was quickly issuing orders.

The commander divided the regiment into three battalions. One, under Capt. Frederick W. Benteen, was to search the river valley for hostiles. Another, under Maj. Marcus A. Reno, was to charge across the river and attack the Indian village there. The third battalion was to advance with Colonel Custer toward the side or rear of the village. Isaiah was assigned to Reno's forces.

"Go quietly. We want to take the village by surprise," he heard an officer say. "The Indians won't know an attack is coming until they feel our bullets."

Isaiah could have told him different. Along the way he had seen signs that the Sioux were watching the troopers. And now they hadn't broken camp and scattered. That meant the Indians were ready for battle and expected to win. "Too many worms," Bloody Knife had said. "Too many Sioux for these soldiers," Isaiah whispered softly to himself.

As he rode reluctantly toward the river with Reno's forces, Isaiah pictured in his mind what was happening in the lodges of the Sioux. Probably many were at their midday meals when the warning came:

"*Woo woo hay-ay hay-ay.* Warriors to your saddles. The white soldiers are now upon us."

The braves would hurry to daub themselves with the red paint of war. They would grab their weapons and leap upon their ponies. They would ride out to meet the soldiers.

Reno's command forded the Little Bighorn River, and the major led out at a gallop through the timber toward the village. Suddenly the woods seemed full of Indians. Some of them had bows and arrows, but most of them had rifles. Isaiah's eyes were blinded by clouds of gunsmoke. His ears were deafened with the crackle of gunfire and the war cries of the Sioux. He was in the thick of battle, and he knew he must defend himself.

Isaiah raised his gun and fired at the Sioux. The Indians fired back, riddling Isaiah's horse with bullets. The dying animal fell over on its back. And Isaiah, tossed to one side, could not get up.

Some of that shower of bullets had hit him. There was a burning in his legs, a burning in his chest. He closed his eyes, and slowly the sounds of battle dimmed.

Hours later, a party of Sioux women searched through the timber for wounded. Behind them rode a heavyset warrior, his sharp eyes sweeping over the battlefield.

Suddenly the women's voices rose in an excited cry, "*Ai-eee*. Come quickly, a *wasicum sapa*, and he is still alive!" The Sioux words meant "black white man." The warrior dismounted and bent over the fallen figure. It was plain to the warrior that this man was mortally wounded. The women's cry aroused Isaiah. Slowly he opened his eyes.

Perhaps he did not know how he had come there. Certainly he did not know that Reno's forces had retreated in defeat and that a few miles away Colonel Custer and every man in his command had died. Isaiah had taken part in the greatest battle in Plains Indian history. More than 3,000 Sioux and their allies had joined together to surprise and destroy the troops who had planned to surprise and destroy them.

Isaiah knew none of that, but as his dazed eyes found the eyes of the warrior who leaned over him, Isaiah did know a friend's face. This was Sitting Bull, great chief of the Sioux. This was a good friend of happier days.

"Bring water," the chief ordered a woman.

She hurried to the river and returned with a water-soaked shawl. She squeezed some water into a horn cup. Sitting Bull held the cup to Isaiah's lips. Painfully Isaiah swallowed a few drops.

The effort brought a new gush of blood from the gaping wound in his chest. He smiled faintly at Sitting Bull. Then Isaiah closed his eyes for the last time, the only member of his race to have died on that battlefield of thousands.

Sitting Bull spoke to the women, "This is the man we call Azimpi. I do not know why he is here with the soldiers. He was always one of us. I knew him as a friend, and once he was afraid of the white soldiers.

His woman is Sioux. When she learns that he has gone to the Sand Hills, she will mourn as the women of our lodges also mourn for their braves killed today."

When Sitting Bull left, the women quickly stripped the buckskin suit from Isaiah's body. One put his white straw hat upon her head. They took his watch and a few other possessions, but out of respect for Sitting Bull, they did not scalp the dead man.

Back at Fort Abraham Lincoln, there came a day of sad reckoning. Clerks made out a report on those slain in the Custer battle. When they reached Isaiah's name they were at a loss, for they knew so little about him.

He had been a sober, industrious man, well liked by everyone. He must have once lived with the Sioux because he had spoken the Sioux language. Some people believed he might have been a runaway slave who had hid out with the Indians. Certainly he had not been seen in the white men's settlements until after the Civil War when the slaves were freed.

But nobody really knew from where he'd come, and nobody knew where he now lay. There was no photograph of him. He had $102.50 army pay due him. The quartermaster did not know to whom to send it.

They could write on their report only what they did know of him, and it was little enough.

They wrote: *Isaiah Dorman. Killed by Indians.*

3. Bob Lemmons: Mustanger

Across the plains a band of thirty beautiful mares galloped into the wind. Their tails streamed out behind them. Their manes lifted like licks of flame. In the lead pounded a powerful stallion, his sharp senses alert for sight or sound or smell of danger.

These were wild horses, running free. They made a magnificent sight, and their like could be found throughout the West.

Behind the band of thirty—a full day's distance behind—rode Bob Lemmons. The herd was unaware of Bob. Not a horse among them had seen him. Nor had Bob seen one of them.

He was following their tracks, and he had studied the tracks of this herd so well that he knew the hoofprints of several horses in it. Even if the herd crossed the tracks of another band, or mingled with other horses, he would not lose these thirty. He meant to capture the herd, and it did not matter how far behind he was. Even five days was not too much. In the end, he would have them.

Bob was a mustanger, a man whose business was capturing the wild horses known as mustangs. An ex-slave, born in 1847, he had grown up with mustangs and known no other life but that of the range and trail. Now he had his own ranch deep in Southwest Texas near the Mexican border. He was the most unusual mustanger in all the West because he could turn *himself* into a mustang! Or at least he could make the mustangs think he was one of them.

Summer lay deep on the land as Bob jogged along on his sorrel mare and watched the ground for tracks of the herd. He enjoyed his work except that sometimes he grew lonesome. Then he talked to the sorrel.

"Rocket, I'd sure like some clean clothes," he told her now. "I feel mighty dirty when I have to wear the same shirt and pants for days."

Rocket twitched her ears to show she had heard.

"I guess you'd like a bath in the creek, too," Bob went on. "But we don't dare change our smell, or the herd will get a whiff of us on the wind. There's nothing like a man-smell to make wild horses stampede. They must be used to our dirty smell by now, though, because their tracks show that they're not scared. Their tracks are smooth as water."

Suddenly Bob pulled the sorrel to a stop.

"Look at that!" he exclaimed. "There's been a fight!"

He dismounted and ran to a nearby patch of ground where the earth had been savagely cut by sharp hoofs. On the trampled grass lay bits of flesh with hair clinging to them. Shrubbery was flattened, and spots of dried blood stained the clumps of weeds.

Bob studied the torn earth. "Stallions fighting," he said. He picked up some small chunks of horseflesh. "A white and a black fighting. See the hairs?" he held out his evidence to Rocket, who had come to stand companionably at her master's side.

"The white won, and he's our stallion," Bob said. "Yes, sir, it's plain as daylight what happened here."

And it was, to Bob's experienced eyes. A stallion is jealous of his mares. If another stallion tries to steal the herd, the old leader will fight him—even to the death. The tracks told Bob that another stallion had come upon the thirty mares and tried to lure them away. He had been attacked and driven off by the herd's leader.

To Bob Lemmons, reading that ground was as

easy as reading a book. He saw that the victor was the one whose tracks he had been following. And the victor had to be the white horse because the victor had chased the other a short distance, apparently nipping chunks from the intruder's rump. Pieces of black-haired flesh dotted the trail of the stranger's flight.

"It was a hard fight," Bob said, "and must have happened just today. The grass hasn't sprung back yet. Our stallion won't be feeling very healthy for a while. That'll make him easier to handle. We'd better start closing in on the herd. It can't be far away, for the fight slowed it down." He mounted the sorrel. "Get along, girl. We've got some horses to catch."

Bob came in sight of the mustangs at sundown. They were on a ridge about a mile away, standing proud and free against the sunset sky.

"Prettiest horses I ever saw," he told Rocket. "And look—there's the white one, the stallion. Whee-dee! What a beauty!"

Cautiously he rode a little nearer.

"This is far enough tonight, Rocket," he said. "We'll ride closer tomorrow. Don't want to get in a hurry and scare our wild herd."

The mustangs were not really wild, of course, not as grizzly bears and mountain lions are wild. Mustangs are descendants of tame horses brought to America by the Spanish. As the years passed, offspring of those first horses escaped from Spanish missions, Indian camps, and western ranches. They gathered in bands and ran free across plains and mountains. In time they turned feral, which means that they had "gone wild," but deep in their nature lay the spirit of the horses who had once served men.

It was a wild mustang, fresh from the northern plains, that Nat Love roped and rode to a championship at Deadwood. Another mustang, captured in the Dakotas and trained for United States Cavalry service, was the only creature left alive on the Custer battlefield that June afternoon when Isaiah Dorman died.

Mustangs opened the trails that led the covered wagons westward. They carried Pony Express riders and pulled stagecoaches. They were the horses of the mountain men and fur trappers and Indians. Without them the cowboys could never have done their work.

When captured, the tough, intelligent mustangs could be gentled into wonderful mounts. The trick was to capture them, and Bob Lemmons knew how to do it.

He worked alone, and he used only the one horse he rode, Rocket. Other mustangers went out together in groups, or at least in pairs, and took with them strings of mounts. By changing to fresh horses often, these mustangers could wear out a herd. Then they captured or, more likely, shot the stallion—that fierce guard and protector of the herd—and drove the tired mares to the ranch corral. The operation took two or three weeks, unless the wily stallion outfoxed them.

A stallion was smart. He knew every inch of the area in which he lived. When mustangers chased his herd, the stallion knew how to lead the herd to safety —between these two giant boulders, perhaps, then up this steep bluff, leap this chasm, race single file through this narrow gorge. The mustangers, lost in a strange country, sometimes went home empty-handed, outwitted by a horse.

Bob Lemmons was never outwitted. He killed no stallions, either. He had too much respect for those noble beasts.

While Bob slept, the white stallion moved his herd. Next morning, Bob ate his breakfast of hardtack —it would never do to build a campfire to cook—and started after the mustangs. At noon he spotted them strung out in a long line and moving at an easy gait across a mesa. He rode up near the end of the string, yet not too close. For the rest of the day he kept that distance as he quietly followed.

For three days he followed, each day drawing a little nearer. The wild horses became used to him, but sometimes the white stallion threw him a puzzled look.

"You've got the right instincts, Big White," Bob sent the horse a silent message. "You think Rocket is just a new mare who has joined your herd, but you

A herd of wild horses. Bob Lemmons, "the most unusual mustanger in the West," could capture an entire herd without killing the leader.

don't understand the bump on her back. Well, I'm the bump."

On the fourth day Bob rode boldly into the heart of the herd. The horses paid no attention to him. They knew his looks and his smell. They accepted him as part of their group. Now Bob decided it was time to drive the stallion from the band so that he could lead the band himself.

The white horse was young and stout-hearted, but he had lost a great deal of blood in his fight. He had a deep cut across one shoulder, and there were many smaller cuts on his body from the strange stallion's teeth and hoofs. Bob counted it lucky that the fight had weakened the horse. As the mares grazed peacefully and the stallion stood apart, on guard, Bob made his move. With a whoop and whirling his lariat like a weapon, he rode at the horse.

Startled, the stallion charged at Bob with high head and stiff-lifted tail. Bob struck at him with the rope. The big horse reared and bared his teeth. His white-rimmed eyes rolled, his ears lay flat. Viciously he lashed out with his forefeet.

Bob's lariat hissed through the air and looped over a hoof. Then Rocket—skilled in felling lassoed longhorn steers and wild horses—swerved quickly, and the stallion crashed to the ground.

He was up in an instant, the rope shaken off,

but the fall had dazed him. Bob swung the lariat like a whip and hit the stallion across the face. The white backed away, blinded for the moment.

Bob followed up his advantage. Still whooping loudly, he slashed again and again at the bewildered mustang. Then Bob pulled his gun from its holster and fired a shot into the air. To the stallion, the noise and the smell of gunpowder meant danger of the worst sort. With a shrill neigh to call the mares, the big horse wheeled and raced off across the plains.

Bob turned and emptied his gun into the air, so that the frightened mares—instead of trying to pass the man and follow their leader—bolted in the other direction. Bob let them bolt. Right now his interest was in the stallion.

"Chase him, girl," he told Rocket.

The mare took off.

Bob had no wish to catch the stallion. He wanted only to drive him far from the herd. He wanted to spare Rocket too, but the mare had once been a wild mustang herself. She was almost a match for the weakened stallion. Time after time the white tried to loop around Bob and return to the herd. Each time Bob sent another volley of shots into the air, and the horse raced ahead again.

Hours passed. Bob was not far behind when the stallion came to the edge of a high steep cliff. For an instant the tired animal hesitated, but the only escape for him was straight down.

He started. Halfway down his hoofs slipped on the rolling gravel. With a scream the big horse fell back on his haunches and slid the rest of the way like a child sliding down a chute.

From the cliff's edge Bob watched anxiously. If the horse broke a leg—but no, he was up. He shook himself, then looked at the man atop the cliff. Bob shot his gun into the air—*bang, bang*. The stallion gave up.

He was beaten. He did not understand how it had happened, but he knew he could never get past the danger on the cliff and return to his mares. Slowly he turned and moved on across the plain. He was not running now. He had lost the fight, but he walked away with dignity.

"You'll be all right, Big White," Bob called after him. "You'll find another herd." He swung Rocket away from the cliff's edge. "We'll rest tonight, girl," he said, "and tomorrow we'll go after our mares."

The nervous mares were bunched not far from where they had bolted. Bob Lemmons rode among them, making himself known as their master and taking command. He acted like a mustang. He not only made the mustangs think he was one of them, he made them think he was the stallion. As the leader, he began to win their confidence. He rounded them up and led them to water. He let them graze. He stood guard, smelling for danger in a way they understood. After a while he began to take them onto new ranges. Once he led them in a stampede.

"I make a pretty good mustang," he told Rocket, chuckling. "Except that I don't eat grass."

Each night he unsaddled his mare while the wild ones watched. He picketed her and slept. No mustang came near him while he slept or while he was afoot.

When the herd was absolutely under his control, Bob led it toward home.

One day on the home ranch, cowboys saw a cloud of dust across the plain. "It's the boss," they said. "He's bringing in a herd."

They opened the corral gates wide.

And Bob, breaking into a gallop, led his herd into the pen. Every mare was in tip-top condition. When groups of mustangers ran a herd down, giving the mares no time to rest or even to eat, the animals often became so weak they could scarcely stand. It was Bob Lemmons's pride that when he brought in a herd of mustangs, every horse was as fresh as the day he had started tracking it.

So only Bob and Rocket were tired. But they knew they had done a good job, and now it was their turn to rest.

4. Cherokee Bill: Outlaw

He rode into the Red Fork Ranch on a bright winter afternoon in 1894, a handsome copper-skinned youth sitting tall and graceful in the saddle. His horse was a fine one, his bridle was silver mounted. His clothes were expensive, and his manners were charming. Although a stranger, he was immediately welcomed by the rancher. Life could be lonely on the scattered ranches in Indian Territory (now Oklahoma), and a pleasant guest was a prize. The visitor explained that he was on his way to the western Panhandle.

"You must stay the night with us," said the rancher. Such hospitality was common in a land where towns were far apart and there were few accommodations for travelers.

Through the afternoon and evening the young visitor was full of high spirits. He entertained the ranch family by singing songs, dancing jigs, telling jokes. They thought him as full of life and the joy of living as anyone who had ever passed that way.

Next morning the youth put on a heavy coat and buckskin gloves, buckled on his gunbelt, and stashed his rifle in its saddle holster. Then with a leap he mounted his horse. The rancher and his family stood on the porch waving good-bye. The guest, in turn, took off his hat and waved farewell as he rode away.

Days later the rancher learned that his lively and gracious visitor was Cherokee Bill, the most feared "badman" in the territory. Bill had a record of robbery and murder unmatched by any other outlaw there, and in those days Indian Territory was home to so many badmen that it was nicknamed "Robbers' Roost" and the "Land of the Six-Shooter."

Cherokee Bill was born in Texas in 1876, of parents who were part black, part white, and part Indian. By the time he was fourteen he had killed his first man—a brother-in-law—in an argument over some hogs, and left home. He rode north to Indian Territory. For a while he worked on ranches, but by his late teens he had made outlawry his way of life. His crimes were so numerous and open that law officers all over the territory were trying to arrest him.

Cherokee Bill killed casually, gaily, and sometimes for no reason other than to practice his marksmanship. Nobody dared challenge him. To protect itself, one town passed a law forbidding anyone to bother him while he was there. That made it a convenient place for Bill to rest up between crimes.

Yet for all his violence, there were those who could say a good word for him. One was S. M. Abbott, who as an old man, many years after Bill was dead, remembered his one meeting with the outlaw.

Abbott had had a farm near Skiatook in Indian Territory, and for a while he was the only white man in the region. One day a skinny fourteen-year-old had come to the farm and asked for food, saying he was starving.

"He was telling the truth," Abbott recalled later. "From the amount of food he put away, he was hungry enough."

After the meal the boy left. Abbott heard no more of him until Bill was known as the worst killer in the country.

By that time Abbott had become fairly prosperous and was the owner of a good horse and a fine saddle. Good horses and fancy saddles were things Cherokee Bill especially liked. Abbott learned that Bill —who was killing and robbing at a great rate—had remarked that there was one horse and saddle in the country that he wanted more than anything he knew. But they belonged to Abbott, he said, so he'd never take them.

Somebody asked him why he had suddenly become so honest.

"Abbott fed me when I was starving," said Cherokee Bill, "and I haven't forgotten it."

"So far as I know, that's about the only good thing Cherokee Bill was ever known to have done," said Abbott, remembering. "But it was enough to convince me that no man sinks so low that there's not a spark of goodness left in him."

Cherokee Bill's life of crime was too easy for him. In time he became careless. Meanwhile, the reward money offered for his capture had grown to $1,300, a sum large enough to tempt others to take risks. A few were tempted to try to capture Bill, but they did not live to collect the reward.

Then Ike Rogers determined to capture Bill. It wasn't reward money that motivated Rogers. Cherokee Bill was courting Rogers's cousin, Maggie Glass. Rogers was a former deputy United States marshal, and it bothered him that the outlaw was seeing his cousin. With other lawmen, he made a plan.

Rogers invited Maggie to his home for a visit, then invited Cherokee Bill. The evening set was January 29, 1895. Later, men wondered why the outlaw had accepted such an invitation. They decided he was saddle-weary, and the prospect of a homecooked meal and seeing Maggie overcame what little caution he still had.

Maggie Glass was not in on the plot, but she suspected a trap. She warned Bill. He laughed.

"If Rogers makes a play, I'll show him how long it takes to commit murder," he told the girl.

It was a tense evening with Rogers and his wife, Maggie Glass, and Cherokee Bill all watching one another warily. A neighbor, Clint Scales, came in. He was part of the plan. The women cooked. The men played cards and talked. Hours passed, yet there never came a moment when Rogers could get the drop on Bill. Finally they all lay down to rest, but nobody slept.

After breakfast, Bill prepared to leave. Rogers, seeing his quarry about to escape, began to grow desperate. Then the outlaw made a mistake. He had rolled a cigarette and did not have a match. So he stooped to the fireplace for a light, and for an instant his head was turned away from Rogers.

In one swift movement Ike Rogers snatched up a piece of firewood and struck the outlaw across the back of the head.

"I must have hit him hard enough to kill an ordinary man, but the blow only knocked Bill down," Rogers told a newspaper reporter later. "Clint and I both jumped on him, but he let out one yell and got to his feet. The three of us tussled for a full twenty minutes before I could get the handcuffs on him."

The two men loaded Cherokee Bill into a wagon and started for the town of Nowata, where deputies were waiting. But Cherokee Bill had not finished fighting. On the way to Nowata he broke his handcuffs and grabbed at Clint Scales's rifle. Scales had to fall out of the wagon to keep his gun, while Rogers—who was riding horseback behind the wagon—kept the outlaw covered until the handcuffs could be replaced. Finally handed over to law officers, Cherokee Bill was taken to the jail at Fort Smith, Arkansas.

There, the presiding judge was Isaac C. Parker, known as the "hanging judge." In his time on the bench in the federal district court in western Arkansas, he sent 88 men to the gallows. When he had come to the Fort Smith court, he had found that Indian Territory, which lay in the court's district, was a lawless land. The stern judge was changing that by making punishment swift and sure for the criminals who stood before him.

Now Cherokee Bill was to be one of them. An armed guard brought Bill to the courtroom in leg shackles. It was a grim place with a few tables and chairs and a gallery for spectators. The judge was equally grim as he sat behind a huge cherrywood desk in a high-backed chair.

Bill had committed many crimes, but he was tried for only one—the murder of an unarmed man in a post office robbery. He was found guilty.

"I sentence you to hang by the neck until you are dead, dead, dead," intoned the judge.

He always repeated the dread word three times. It was not that he was cruel, for he was known to be a very fair man. He only wanted to warn the lawless that law had come to Indian Territory. He knew that deputy United States marshals risked their lives over and over in capturing outlaws and bringing them to Fort Smith. It was his duty to see that justice was done. People who knew the judge swore that he had never sent an innocent man to his death nor let a guilty man go free.

Cherokee Bill was guilty. There was no doubt about that.

Yet he had still not finished fighting. While awaiting an appeal of his case, he managed to get hold of a revolver and stage a jailbreak. Cornered, he began a sniping match with guards. Every time he fired, he "gobbled." It was an eerie, throaty sound halfway between the bark of a coyote and the cry of a turkey cock. It was an Indian threat; when an Indian gobbled he meant to kill someone within hearing.

Cherokee Bill was part Indian. He gobbled, and a guard died from a bullet in the stomach.

The hanging of Cherokee Bill. The ruthless outlaw "had a record of robbery and murder unmatched by any other bandit in Indian Territory."

Subdued at last, Bill was chained in his cell, and his fighting days were over. He never got another chance.

On a March day in 1896, he walked quietly to a scaffold made of rough lumber. In sentencing him, Judge Parker had called Bill a "ferocious monster" who had taken the lives of all who stood in his way. He said Bill's record was the worst of any criminal he had known, and he was sorry there was not a harsher punishment to give him. The judge talked quite a while.

Not so Bill. As he stood on the scaffold, he was asked if he had anything to say to the crowd that had gathered to watch the execution.

"No," answered Cherokee Bill. "I came here to die, not to make a speech." He was soon dead.

Cherokee Bill and his kind, whether black or white, were violent men who thrived in the lawless atmosphere of the Old West. And yet, in a strange way, they themselves brought about the end of an era. Their violence was so extreme that they made the need for an orderly judicial process more pressing. And so, largely because of them, law came more quickly to the prairies!

5. Willis Peoples: Wolf Hunter

They called the big gray prairie wolf "Old Two Toes" because he had lost part of a front foot in a trap. Nobody in the frontier town of Meade, on Crooked Creek in Kansas, felt sorry about the wolf's foot. They were only sorry that he had gotten out of the trap at all, because he was a killer.

He pulled down and killed full-grown cows. He mangled sheep and ranch dogs and bit open the throats of calves. Sometimes, for the sport of it, he nipped off a calf's tail. There was many a bob-tailed calf around Crooked Creek. In the year of 1882, the big wolf ruled the range along the bluffs and sand hills where cattle fed, and he cost the ranchers big sums of money in slaughtered livestock. They hated him.

He couldn't be trapped, poisoned, or shot. He was too smart. Since the injury to his foot, he had avoided traps. He ignored the poisoned meat put out to tempt him, and no one could get close enough to shoot him. It was rare for anyone to get close enough even to see him. But when ranchers came across the tracks of a wolf with a damaged front paw, they knew that Old Two Toes had been around looking for another fine feast.

Then the lobo—as wolves were sometimes called —took a mate. She was a large wolf, black and fierce.

Hunting together, the savage pair was soon attacking horses and even range bulls.

The ranchers grew desperate. They held "wolf meetings" to decide what to do. They offered a bounty, a reward for anyone who could destroy Old Two Toes. They hired professional hunters, and these wolfers brought in dogs trained to track and kill.

None of it did any good. The bounty hunters failed. The professional wolfers and their dogs followed the lobos from herd to herd. They saw many slain cattle and plenty of Old Two Toes's tracks, but they only once glimpsed the killers. Finally the wolfers left.

Some of the ranchers wondered if they would have to leave, too. Ranch profits were not large. The loss of so much livestock could wipe out those profits. Small ranchers began to fear they might go broke.

Matters couldn't have been much worse on the day Willis Peoples came to town and heard the ranchers talking about their trouble. Willis Peoples was in the cattle business himself, one of the few black ranchers in the West. He owned a small place south of Meade. He listened gravely to the anxious talk about the wolf. Then he made the men at Meade an offer. He said if they would leave Old Two Toes and his mate alone for one month, he would guarantee to bring in the killer.

"How can you do it?" one rancher asked.

"I'll camp on the trail of those wolves night and day," Peoples said. "I'll live with them until they've got their paws up in the air begging forgiveness."

Some of the ranchers laughed. Some said that Peoples didn't know how smart Old Two Toes was. Some said the whole idea was ridiculous. But the ranchers who knew Willis Peoples believed him.

"We've tried everything else and failed," they said. "Let's see what Peoples can do."

In the end, the cattlemen agreed to Peoples's plan. He told them they must keep him supplied with food, water, and fresh horses. They could bring the supplies to him from the ranch nearest where he was each day. And he said they must look after his place while he was away. That settled, he mounted his horse and left for the ranch where Old Two Toes was reported to have made his latest kill.

Soon Peoples found the tracks of the lobos and started on their trail. Leaning from the saddle, he watched for every bare patch of ground where a footprint might show. It was slow, wearying work, but he was a patient man. Day after day, from first light until it was too dark to see, he followed the faint tracks of the killers. A week passed. Then another.

The wolves knew he was after them. Peoples wanted them to know. Unlike Bob Lemmons on the mustang trail, Peoples wanted to keep the wolves uneasy and on the move. He could never quite overtake them, but neither did he give them enough time to rest or hunt for food.

After two weeks Peoples found himself following only Old Two Toes's misshapen tracks. He knew the reason for that. The tired, hungry she-wolf had had enough of the chase, and she'd deserted her mate. A few evenings later Peoples suddenly came upon Old Two Toes killing a calf.

The hungry wolf had no time to enjoy a meal, however, for Peoples went after him. Unluckily, the horse Peoples was riding had gone lame that day and could not run. The wolf escaped, his gray coat soon lost from Peoples's view in the gray shadows of twilight. The next day, on a fresh mount, the hunter took up the trail again.

Old Two Toes began to tire. As the days passed,

Lobos—the timber wolves of the West. When Willis Peoples went wolf hunting, he camped on the trail of the clever beasts night and day.

his trail became plainer and easier to follow. He no longer tried to hide his tracks by walking on rock ledges or matted grass, or by doubling back wolf-fashion on the trail. Now Peoples did not have to lean so far from the saddle while straining his eyes for dim prints.

An afternoon came when the tracks led into a canyon, and it looked to Willis Peoples as if the wolf was almost crawling. The man loosened his gun in its holster and rode cautiously. He knew he was nearing the end of the long hunt. Suddenly he spotted his prey.

The lobo was a hundred feet in front of him, crouched for protection under a high clay bank. Hunter and hunted stared at each other, the man's eyes wary and the wolf's eyes red with hate. Peoples dismounted, keeping his rifle ready for a quick shot if the wolf attacked. A killer was a killer. Desperation could give him unexpected strength and speed.

Slowly Peoples walked toward the beast. But the old wolf only watched, his ears twitching. Was it possible that the wolf had actually given up the fight? Peoples wondered.

At fifty feet, he stopped, for his horse had smelled the wolf and grown nervous. The horse pulled wildly at the end of the reins which Peoples had wrapped around his right arm. Peoples spoke to quiet the horse. Then he raised his gun and took careful aim at the wolf's head.

"You're my fair game," he whispered as he pulled the trigger.

Next day Willis Peoples rode into Meade with Old Two Toes's carcass. Men flocked around him. They stretched the wolf's body in the street and measured it—seven feet! A huge wolf, with a mangled front paw. Old Two Toes, done for at last.

The happy ranchers congratulated Peoples. "But how did you know you could catch him when even the wolfers gave up?" they asked.

Willis Peoples tried to explain. "That wolf represented *bad*," he said. "He was bad for this community. Killing him would be good for the community. I didn't know just how I'd do it but I did know that any man with his mind made up is a majority. My mind was made up to get that wolf. And that's how it was."

6. Bill Pickett: Cowhand

Bill Pickett was a fine cowhand, but he was more than a cowhand. He was a living legend in the Old West and one of the first international rodeo stars. When he was chosen for the National Rodeo Hall of Fame his citation began: "Bill Pickett's name is immortal."

Pickett began his cowboying down in the mesquite country of South Texas, where he was born not long after the Civil War. He grew up a big-handed, wild-riding fellow, and he invented the daring sport of steer wrestling.

Pickett didn't call it a sport. To him it was simply the quickest way to handle an unruly steer who had broken from the herd and run into the brush where a cowboy couldn't use a lariat.

He didn't call his invention "wrestling," either. He called it "bulldogging" because, like a bulldog, he used his teeth.

Here is one account of Pickett's bulldogging:

The way Bill Pickett went at it, he piled out of his saddle onto the head of a running steer, sometimes jumping five or six feet to tie on. He'd grab a horn in each hand and twist them till the steer's nose came up. Then he'd reach in and grab the steer's upper lip with his strong white teeth, throwing up his hands to show he wasn't holding any more, and fall to one side of the steer, dragging along beside him till the animal went down.

It made an impressive spectacle, all right! Bill Pickett was admired by his hard-riding comrades on the range, but none of them cared to attempt his feat. It wasn't until he went to work for Colonel Zack Miller, who owned the vast 101 Ranch in western Oklahoma, that fame came Pickett's way. Miller called Pickett the "greatest sweat-and-dirt cowhand that ever lived—bar none," and when the colonel put together a rodeo he made Pickett one of the performers. Another cowboy in the show was Will Rogers, who at times worked on

Bill Pickett, "the greatest sweat-and-dirt cowhand that ever lived," invented the art of bulldogging.

the 101. He was a good man with a lariat, and he later became world-famous as a humorist and an actor.

The rodeo was an instant success. First thing Bill Pickett knew, he was no longer herding cattle. Instead, he was traveling with the show to cities all over the United States, to Canada, to South America. His "act" was bulldogging; it always amazed and fascinated the spectators. In England Pickett performed for the king and queen and dined with an earl in his castle.

On the rodeo program he was billed as "The Wonderful Bill Pickett," and wherever he went he was the star—the hit of the show!

Then one December night in 1908 in Mexico City, 25,000 people bought tickets to a bullfight, expecting to see Bill Pickett die in the ring. Somehow Miller and Pickett had gotten involved in a $5,000 wager that Pickett could tackle bare-handed a fighting Spanish bull. To the Mexicans, the wager was like a national insult. How could a mere cowboy from the United States do what no great Mexican matador would dare attempt? The gringo would most assuredly be killed, and it would serve him right!

The Mexicans made up some ugly rules for the contest between an unarmed man and a bull bred to fight and kill. Pickett was to go up against the bull without the prefight help always given to matadors, who fought with swords. For Pickett there would be no lancemen on horseback to take the bull's first charges and tire it, and there would be no men to send barbed shafts into the bull's shoulders and thus weaken it by loss of blood. And the rules said that Pickett must be in direct physical contact with the bull for five full minutes. Gamblers were betting he would live no longer than four. Pickett knew the danger, but his fighting blood was aroused.

The Mexicans prepared for the cowboy's death

by bringing a coffin into the arena. *"Viva el toro!"* they shouted. "Long live the bull!"

The bull chosen was a mean one called "Little Bean" because of his strangely spotted skin. When the arena gate was opened, out roared Little Bean, and from the other side of the arena came Pickett on his treasured horse Spradley.

Little Bean snorted and charged. Spradley knew all about mean animals. At the last second he took a dancing sidestep, and the bull rushed past. Spradley started to give chase, but the bull did not run away as a longhorn steer would have done. Little Bean was a fighter. He wheeled and charged again. The surprised Spradley sidestepped nimbly, and again the bull rushed past. Twice more the bull charged and overshot.

Pickett grew worried. He could not swing onto the bull when it kept wheeling. He realized the horse must stand still in order to draw the bull into position, but Pickett wanted none of that. He rode to the barricade and called to Miller, "A pony's going to die before I can get close enough. I can't risk Spradley."

The Mexicans thought he was giving up. *"Cobarde!"* they shouted angrily. "Coward!"

"Go back in there, Bill, and get that bull," Zack Miller urged. "If you don't, they're going to get all of us!"

Without a word, Pickett rode back into the ring,

In Colonel Zack Miller's rodeo, the daring bulldogger was billed as "The Wonderful Bill Pickett." He is seen here on his famous horse Spradley.

but the watching 101 Ranch hands saw that his face was tense with concern for Spradley.

Little Bean charged. Before the horse could sidestep, Pickett pulled him up short. The bull's horns tore into the horse's rump. As Spradley screamed, Pickett slid off his back and onto the bloody horns. Little Bean tried to gore the horse again, but the limping Spradley got out of the danger zone.

Now the bull turned its attention to Pickett, who was hanging onto its horns for dear life.

Little Bean, head tossing, raced across the bullring. Pickett dug his heels into the ground, but the bull didn't even slow down. It threw Pickett against a wall. It dropped to its knees and tried to pin him into the dirt with its horns. It whipped him back and forth as though he were an empty sack.

"Bill's being murdered," Zack Miller yelled, "and it's only been two minutes!"

But Bill Pickett lived up to his description. He was "wonderful." He wrapped his arms around the bull's neck, and fastened his wrists under its throat. He pulled up his legs, and pressed his knees against Little Bean's nostrils.

"The hold was Bill's favorite," a 101 puncher said later, "and no four-footed creature had ever withstood it."

Nor did Little Bean. He began to weaken.

But this was not what the fans had paid to see. The cowboy must die!

They began to throw bottles at Pickett, and their aim was good. His hold on the horns loosened.

"It's been six minutes!" Zack Miller shouted. "They're not going to ring that stop bell!"

With a rush, 101 hands rode into the ring and roped the bull's hind legs. The spectators, furious with disappointment, threw everything they could find to throw. The president of Mexico, who was there, called out a group of soldiers to restore order and guard the cowboys. The empty coffin was hauled out of the arena.

In the end, Spradley's wound healed. Pickett recovered from three broken ribs. Miller collected the wager, and the 101 Ranch Rodeo went home for Christmas.

When World War I began, the rodeo was in England. Its horses were conscripted for English army service, and the show closed.

Gradually time caught up with the 101 Ranch. It fell on bad days and much of it was sold to pay off debts. Zack Miller grew old and ill.

By then Pickett too was an old man. He had his own ranch of 160 acres, but he spent much time with Miller. It was to please the ailing Miller that Pickett went out one March day to rope a skittish horse. The horse kicked Pickett in the head. Eleven days later the cowboy died of a fractured skull, while Miller sat at the bedside, where he had kept a constant vigil. On the day of the cowboy's death, Zack Miller wrote some verses in memory of Pickett. They were the simply put lines of an old man mourning a lost friend, and among them were these:

Like many men in the old-time West,
On any job, he did his best.
He left a blank that's hard to fill
For there'll never be another Bill.

By the time Bill Pickett died, the Old West was gone. But Pickett had known it at its best, and he had been one of its best.

7.   The Soldiers

The Indians called the black cavalrymen "buffalo soldiers" because the troopers had thick curly hair. Also the black troopers wore buffalo skin coats during winter campaigns.

But now it was a summer day—August 16, 1881. The troopers wore the blue uniform of the Ninth United States Cavalry as they rested at their camp in the little New Mexico town of Canada Alamosa. The buffalo soldiers were just back from a hard chase after hostile Apache Indians. They had earned their rest, but they did not call it resting. In cavalryman talk, they were "letting their saddles cool."

Suddenly the drum of hoofbeats and an agonized shout broke the quiet of the summer morning. Up the canyon raced a rider. "My wife! My children! Dead! All dead!" he cried.

His words brought villagers rushing from their adobe houses. Men of the Ninth hurried from their quarters. Some of the soldiers ran down the road to meet the rider. He was a Mexican whose ranch lay a few miles down the canyon.

"Apaches!" he gasped as he slid from his sweating horse. "They killed my wife and children! They're on the way here to attack the town! It's Nana!"

In a moment all was fear and excitement in little Canada Alamosa. For Nana was the ferocious old leader of a group of Apache braves, and Apaches were the most dangerous Indian tribe in all the West. They hated the whites who had taken their land. Bands of fearless warriors, determined to drive the whites away, terrorized frontier settlements. Equally determined to protect the settlers, the Ninth Cavalry was always ready to pursue the Apaches.

"Saddle up!" commanded Lt. George Burnett, the troopers' white officer. In a few moments he led a detachment of fifteen troopers down the canyon road. At the ranch they found the horribly mutilated bodies of a woman and three children.

Grim-faced, the soldiers set out to follow the Indians' trail through the rugged country of sharp cliffs and flat-topped hills. The trail lay plain across a dry creek bottom, over a mesa dotted with bunch grass, and up a ridge. From there they spied the raiders a mile away, driving a herd of horses toward the nearby Cuchilla Negra Mountains. The cavalrymen peered across the sunbaked land.

"They're Apaches, all right, about eighty of them," one said.

Riding swiftly, they overtook the Indians in the rock-strewn foothills. But the Apaches were ready for them. The Indians had spread out and hidden among the big rocks in order to encircle the troopers. Crouched in a crevice, old Nana smiled as he watched the unsuspecting cavalrymen ride into the trap. He spat in the dust to show his contempt for them. Then he raised one lean brown fist and waved it in the air.

That was the signal for his warriors. Quickly they darted from rock to rock to close the circle. Soon they had the troopers pinned in a pocket with no way out. The soldiers poured gunfire at their unseen captors. Nana spat in the dust again.

Now the Indians waited. They would let the soldiers shoot until they ran out of ammunition, and then move in for the kill.

The cavalrymen were in a desperate situation. They needed reinforcements quickly or not one of them would be left alive. But who could get through the hostile lines? Trooper John Rogers volunteered.

A storm of Apache bullets swept around Rogers as his plunging horse broke through the circle of Indians. The horse staggered as a bullet creased its hip, but the gallant animal raced on. To the watching soldiers it seemed a miracle that Rogers was not killed.

Now time dragged for the trapped men. Overhead a pitiless sun beat down, almost blinding them with its white glare. Their rifles grew slippery in their sweating hands. They could hear the faint scratch of pebbles as their enemy crept nearer. Then Apache bullets began to strike dangerously close, zinging off rocks and kicking up dust clouds. The troopers flattened themselves against the ground and behind rocks.

"Save your fire," the lieutenant ordered, "and if help doesn't come, be ready to die—" Suddenly he stopped. He had started to say "be ready to die to the last man." He realized that wasn't necessary. No man would risk becoming an Apache captive. Quick death was far better.

All at once the shooting broke off. The startled cavalrymen looked at one another, a question in their eyes. What new tricks were the Apaches up to?

Cautiously, some of the men peered over the rocks. The Indians had left. They were swarming toward a little hill a quarter of a mile away. One man climbed a rock for a better look. Then he saw it. A small detachment of the Ninth was rounding the hill!

"It's Lieutenant Valois!" he shouted. "John Rogers reached camp!"

A cheer went up from the soldiers. Then another man exclaimed, "Valois is in trouble! They're attacking him!"

With a rush the troopers made for their horses. As they left the rocks, they saw that the eighty Apaches had attacked the rescue group. Many cavalry horses were down. Several soldiers lay wounded, and the others were jumping from their horses and scurrying for shelter behind a few large prairie dog mounds, the only cover they could reach. Not far away, the Indians were gathering to attack again.

Lieutenant Burnett's men charged past the Indians at a gallop. Straight to Valois's broken line they rode. Dismounting, they sent volley after volley toward the Indians. Their steady fire kept the Apaches pinned back while Valois got his wounded into the timbered hill to the rear.

"Fall back!" The order came from Valois, and the whole line of troopers began to move back to a better position in the timber.

But four of Valois's men did not hear the order. Off to one side and unseen, they were left behind. When they discovered their plight, it was too late to make a run for the timber alone.

"Lieutenant, don't leave us!" one called.

Valois was already too far to the rear. He did not hear. Lieutenant Burnett and his men did hear the cry for help. They knew that, left there alone, the four stranded men would be butchered by the foe.

"Who'll help in a rescue?" the lieutenant shouted.

Two men volunteered—Sgt. Moses Williams and Pvt. Augustus Walley.

The lieutenant ordered the other troopers to crawl to safety in the rear. He, Williams, and Walley would try to stand off the Indians. Already the Apaches were moving toward the four helpless cavalrymen.

Using what protection they could find in a sparse cover of bushy piñons, the three rescuers aimed careful shots into the Indian ranks. Their bullets kept the Indians at a distance while two of the threatened soldiers ran to safety. But a third man was wounded; he could not get up.

"It's my bunky!" Walley exclaimed. "I'll get him!"

Burnett nodded. "We'll try to cover you."

Walley ran back to his picketed horse, mounted, and raced to his fallen bunkmate. Jumping from his horse, he lifted the wounded man into the saddle, then leaped up behind him and galloped safely to the rear. The Indians had not fired. They wanted the officer.

Now the fourth man struggled to his feet and wandered off in the direction of the enemy. It was plain that he was badly rattled. Old Nana, eyes glittering,

The rescue of a fallen comrade. The annals of the buffalo soldiers are filled with stories of heroism.

stepped from a cluster of Indians and beckoned the dazed man to come closer. Lieutenant Burnett raced for his horse.

Galloping after the soldier, Burnett wheeled his horse between the man and the Indians while Sergeant Williams fired rapidly at the Indians.

An Apache cry went up, and the warriors tried desperately to fell Lieutenant Burnett. In their excitement they shot wildly. Twice they hit his horse, but Burnett safely guided the soldier back to his own lines.

The fight was not over. It lasted until nightfall. A few Apaches were slain, and the rest disappeared in the darkness. At daybreak the weary soldiers began to follow the Indians' trail again, but at the Mexican border they had to turn back. It was unlawful for American troops to cross the border so Nana had only to lead his warriors across to find safety.

Now it was August 17, 1881, and by evening the troopers were back in camp, letting their saddles cool. To them it had been just another day's work. But later Sergeant Williams, Private Walley, and Lieutenant Burnett would each be presented with the nation's highest military award, the Congressional Medal of Honor, for valor above and beyond the call of duty in the Battle of the Cuchilla Negra Mountains.

The Ninth was one of two black cavalry regiments. The other was the Tenth. Both were organized in 1866 and 1867 soon after the Civil War, and they did the same kind of work.

During that war, the Indians throughout the West had grown bold. To them the Civil War meant little. They knew nothing of the struggle to free the slaves and to preserve the Union. When the army withdrew most of its western troops to fight in the war, the Indians thought this was a sign of cowardice.

"The white soldiers are afraid of us. They have run away," the warriors said scornfully around their council fires. So the confident Indians stepped up their attacks on frontier settlements.

After the Civil War, the army needed to rebuild its strength in the West to stop the Indian raids. Yet so many regular troops had been killed and wounded in the war, or were simply tired of fighting, that there were not enough recruits for western duty. The army turned to the ex-slaves and asked them to enlist. Many whites believed this was a mistake, for they thought black men would not make good soldiers. These whites ignored the good record of the 180,000 black soldiers who had served the Union army in the Civil War. Of them 33,380 had given their lives for freedom and Union. Other blacks had served with honor in the American Revolution and the War of 1812.

Despite white fears, the army decided to "experiment" with black troops, and the two regiments were formed. For the black men it was a chance to start a new life, a chance to prove themselves as free men. They enlisted in such large numbers that, at one time, forty per cent of the Indian-fighting army was made up of black soldiers.

Congress provided that all officers of the new regiments were to be white. At first the army could find no officers willing to take assignments with the Ninth and Tenth Cavalries. Fortunately the two commanding officers they finally got—Col. Edward Hatch and Col. Benjamin H. Grierson—were dedicated men who believed wholeheartedly in their black regiments.

The buffalo soldiers of the Tenth Cavalry served their country "with honor and distinction." These scenes in the field were drawn by artist Frederic Remington.

There were fine lesser officers too. Among them was John J. Pershing, who was later to become commander-in-chief of the American Expeditionary Forces in World War I.

The exception to the rule was Lt. Henry O. Flipper, an officer assigned to the Tenth Cavalry. He was the first black graduate of West Point, the United States Military Academy.

The Ninth and Tenth Cavalries were lucky in their officers, but in little else. They got the worst, most run-down forts in which to live, and the poorest food to eat. They were issued the oldest equipment, much of it castoffs from more favored regiments. Their horses were usually worn-out, trail-weary nags. Even their regimental banners were homemade, faded, and worn—flags quite unlike the silk-embroidered standard supplied by headquarters to white regiments.

Despite poor conditions the black soldiers continued to serve loyally, and their rate of desertion was far lower than in white regiments.

They served, with bravery and honor, from the Mississippi River to the Rocky Mountains, and from Canada to Mexico. To them fell many of the longest marches, the most grueling campaigns.

They fought Ute Indians in Colorado, and Cheyennes and Arapahoes in Kansas. For years they were the only military force in West Texas, where

Comanches and Kiowas were trying to make the Staked Plains a graveyard for white settlers.

In New Mexico and Arizona they marched thousands of miles under nearly impossible conditions to control marauding Apaches and Kickapoos. In the final year of the Plains Wars, 1891, they took a major part in quelling the last uprising of the once-mighty Sioux.

When they were not after Indians, the buffalo troops had other duties. They escorted stagecoaches and cattle herds. They fought Mexican bandits and western outlaws. They scouted for horse thieves and built forts. They patrolled and mapped thousands of miles of uncharted country. They protected railroad workers and white settlements.

In western towns they often faced the hostility of the very people they guarded. Many settlers had been Southern sympathizers during the Civil War. They had no love for the Union, the army, or the black race. Being a buffalo soldier in such places was a thankless job. The troopers got little credit for their labors, or even for their heroism.

There were many heroes. A dozen cavalrymen of the Ninth and Tenth won the Congressional Medal of Honor. The first to be honored was leather-hard Sgt. Emanuel Stance who stood five feet, six inches in his cavalry boots. He was awarded the medal in 1870 for saving a wagon train from Kickapoo Indians. The tough little man wept openly as he received the highest military honor his country could bestow.

Yet the heroic deeds of most troopers were never known beyond the campfires of their comrades and their foes. The Indians knew the worth of the buffalo soldier. Like the buffalo itself, he had strength and courage. The Tenth Cavalry, proud of the nickname, put the figure of a buffalo in its regimental emblem.

Another who knew the worth of the troopers was Frederic Remington, the great painter of the frontier West. He rode with a unit of the Tenth on patrol in Arizona and was in Dakota when the Ninth fought the last engagement with the Sioux. His paintings of both regiments are among our finest pictorial records of the Plains Wars.

And their officers knew the troopers' worth. In report after report to army headquarters, the officers made it plain that the "experiment" had been a success.

Most important of all, the buffalo soldiers knew their own worth. They knew they were no play-day soldiers who deserted when the life was hard. Their honorable scars proved they were brave men serving their country. Why did they serve, when there was so little glory or money in it? "Oh, we like it," they said quietly. It was an answer that meant much. It meant they were soldiers who knew the proud feeling of doing a soldier's duty, and they found it good.

8.   The Cowboys

Oh say little dogies, when are
you going to lie down
And quit this forever shifting around?
My horse is leg-weary and
I'm mighty tired.

On and on Bose Ikard sang, crooning the "cow lullaby" that usually soothed a restless herd at night and persuaded it to lie down and sleep. His herd needed sleep. So did Ikard. The black cowboy had been in the saddle almost constantly for three days and nights. As the song said, he was mighty tired.

All the cowboys on this trail drive in the spring of 1867 were tired. For weeks they had been pushing 2,000 longhorn steers up the cattle trail to markets in the north, and they'd had some bad times.

Their herd of half-wild Texas cattle had been panicked by thunderstorms, mired in rain-soaked ground, and attacked by Indians. Every night for the past three nights the steers had been frightened by Comanches trying to stampede the herd and make off with some of the cattle. Now the animals were so nervous they milled around in the dark and refused to bed down, no matter how much Ikard sang.

"You're wasting your music," a voice said from the darkness. Col. Charles Goodnight, the Texas rancher who owned the herd, rode up to Ikard. He and the young cowboy had been on guard during the night. "These steers aren't going to settle," the older man said. "Between us and the Comanches, we've shot them to pieces. They're jumpy as jack rabbits."

Ikard nodded. "They've had a hard time ever since the drive started."

"It's been a jinxed trip," Goodnight agreed. "But if the Indians will leave us alone, we'll still make it to Colorado and get a good price for these beefs from the goldminers. Those men need meat." He glanced toward the east, where the sky was beginning to grow light. "It's almost dawn. I'll ride up to camp and wake the boys. We can move out early."

"I'll keep an eye on things here," Ikard said, and settled back in his saddle.

It was the hour he liked best, when the first

cheeping birds awakened and a fresh morning breeze rippled the long grass of the prairie. His eyes swept over the herd, and he saw that the cattle had grown fairly quiet. Yes, he thought, it was a peaceful hour with the night's work done and a good breakfast coming up. He sighed contentedly. Nothing to do now, he told himself, except wait for the cook's call.

He was wrong. But he could not know what was about to happen.

When Goodnight rode into camp, which was situated well ahead of the herd, he tied his horse to a wheel of the cook's chuck wagon and walked toward the sleeping cowboys. They were stretched out on the ground around the wagon. Suddenly something happened—perhaps an owl hooted, perhaps a brisk gust of wind rattled the branches of a cottonwood tree—and in an instant several steers jumped to their feet, their eyes wide with fear.

It doesn't take many steers to start a stampede. The fright of one animal can be sensed by the others. Then panic whips like a flash of lightning through the whole herd. It happened now.

The danger erupted so quickly that Goodnight had no time to rouse the sleeping men. Fear-maddened animals were stampeding right down on the camp, and at full speed. It looked as if the men would be trampled to death.

Goodnight snatched a blanket from a snoring puncher and jumped in front of the steers. Shouting and waving his blanket, he managed to split the herd around the wagon and men. Startled cowboys awoke and scrambled up. When the herd had passed, the men ran for their picketed horses. Goodnight jerked his horse's tie-rope from the wagon wheel, swung into the saddle, and raced after the longhorns. If they weren't stopped, they could run themselves to death.

The way to stop stampeding cattle was to get at the front of the herd and turn the animals to one side, so that they ran back in the direction from which they had come. It was called "circling" and once the cattle were running in a circle the riders could control them.

Now Goodnight raced to get to the front.

And where was Bose Ikard?

Relaxed and peaceful, Ikard had been waiting for the breakfast call and keeping a mild eye on the herd, when the stampede began with the force of an explosion. In the half-light of dawn, all the astonished Ikard could see was a panicked throng of 2,000 cattle plunging past him. Swiftly he rode down the side of the bolting animals to the head of the herd.

Of all the dangers that cowboys faced, a stampede was the worst. Riding pell-mell alongside crazed longhorns, with the ground under his horse's hoofs cut by banks and prairie dog holes, took a desperate sort of courage. Ikard rode. But he made no move to turn the cattle.

Then as the last darkness faded, and it became light enough to see, the cowboy glanced back over his shoulder. He saw Goodnight pounding down the line on his big cowpony, Charlie. Instantly Ikard shot across the front of the herd and threw the lead steers around. In a few moments the cattle were circled and slowing down.

The panting colonel galloped up to his best rider.

"Bose, why in tarnation didn't you turn them sooner?" he demanded.

"I'll tell you," said the cautious Ikard with a wry smile. "I wasn't sure who had this herd until I saw you. I thought maybe the Indians had it, and I wasn't going to help the Indians steal our cattle."

Goodnight threw back his head and laughed. "Trust Bose!" he said to nobody in particular. "Trust Bose not to lend the Comanches a hand!"

Breakfast was sketchy that morning because the stampeding steers had scattered the cook's supplies, but by full sunup they were ready to move out. They'd had a bad few minutes. Now it was over and already half-forgotten, for on the trail there was little time to think about past dangers.

Young though he was, barely 20 years old, Bose

Ikard was a cowboy who could be trusted for more than not helping Indian raiders. He was not only the best rider in the outfit, he was Charles Goodnight's right-hand man. He was the colonel's detective, even his banker. Ikard carried the cash on the trail, and it sometimes amounted to thousands of dollars. He laughed at the thought of being robbed. Who would look in *his* bedroll for money? Everybody knew that cowpokes spent their money as fast as they got it!

"I have trusted him farther than any living man," Goodnight often said of his young friend. "He was the most skilled and trustworthy man, and he surpassed any man I knew in endurance and stamina. There was a dignity about him that was wonderful."

Bose Ikard was born a slave in Mississippi and was brought West by his owners when he was five. He grew up on the Texas range, where he learned to handle cattle and fight Indians. At nineteen, a freed man, he joined Goodnight's outfit and so began a lifelong association that stood both men in good stead. Goodnight credited Ikard with saving Goodnight's life on several occasions when they were out in wild country and threatened by outlaws or hostile Indians. In turn, the rancher gave the younger man good business advice so that in time Ikard had his own Texas ranch.

Ikard died in January of 1929 and Goodnight—well into his nineties—died in December of the same year. Shortly before his death the rancher had a granite marker erected on Ikard's grave, inscribed with his personal tribute to Bose Ikard and signed, "C. Goodnight."

Ikard had grown up in the West and learned his trade, but there were other ex-slaves who went to the West after the Civil War. In the South especially, the newly freed men had a bitter time earning even the most meager living. But on the vast plains beyond the Mississippi River, a better life awaited men who had the will and strength to make the westward trek. Thousands of ex-slaves made it. On foot, on horseback, by wagon train they went. Many had had experience handling horses in the South. They sought jobs on ranches. Eventually there were probably close to 5,000 black cowboys on the western frontier.

There was less discrimination on the open ranges than anywhere else in the West for all these ex-slaves. It would be untrue to say there was none, but usually the demands of the job overcame prejudice. A cowboy was a "man with work to do." How well he did that work was the yardstick by which his comrades measured him. A "top-hand" puncher, whatever his color, was a top man in any outfit.

There was an economic aspect, too. Where there are more jobs than men there is less discrimination. There were plenty of range jobs in the West. Over a period of twenty-five years, millions of cattle were driven up the trails. In the single summer of 1871, some 700,000 cattle were herded to Kansas cow towns. There were never enough good cowboys to fill the waiting jobs.

Often the first work a new westerner found was rounding up wild cattle in Texas. Out in the brush country hundreds of thousands of longhorns roamed free. They belonged to nobody, for during the four years of war there had been no cowboys riding the ranges and keeping track of the herds. The cattle had wandered where their noses led them, and they had turned ferocious.

After them went the new cowboys. One was Henry Becker, a puncher who could find cattle in thickets so dense he could see only a few yards ahead. He located animals by sniffing the air for their scent and listening for the sounds of big beasts moving through the brush.

Since a man could smell and hear as well in the dark as in daylight, Henry often rode at night. His friends nicknamed him "The Coyote" because coyotes, too, hunt at night. In his saddlebags he carried dried beef and cornbread, and he mixed the juice of hot chili peppers in his coffee. He got out of the habit of talking because he hunted alone so much, but he knew how to find wild cattle and drive them onto the range.

Most cowboys who rode the Old West are now nameless. But a few, like Becker, had a skill so great or

A group of black cowboys from Bonham, Texas. All over the West black men won the respect and admiration of their comrades on the trail.

a style so unique that they are remembered today. Many an area has its story of such a special cowboy and many of these special cowboys were freeborn black men or ex-slaves. Tony Williams was the star of one story.

With an early-day trail crew, Williams was trying to cross the flooded Red River. All the steers were strung out behind him as he rode a mule through the turbulent water. In midstream a great wave knocked him from his mule. The mule swam on, the herd swam on, but Williams disappeared under the water.

"We thought he had drowned," one of his friends said later. "But in a little while we discovered him holding on to the tail of a big steer. When the steer went up the bank, Tony was still holding on and went right up with him!"

Life as a cowboy had many such strange experiences, as the new cowboys learned—and learned quickly. For as soon as the wild cattle had been rounded up by riders like Becker, ranchers had to get the herds to a market. There was no place to sell beef in Texas, but there were plenty of markets in eastern cities, and in northern mining camps, Indian reservations, and military posts. The only way to move cattle to those places was to drive them every step of the many miles from Texas to Kansas railroad towns, where steers could be shipped east, or still farther north to Colorado and Wyoming.

So the cattle trails were laid out, trail crews were hired, and the long drives began. "On the hoof overland," the crews called them.

Life for the trail cowboys became a string of hot dusty days and tense sleepless nights of hard work, but they had a saying on the range that nobody ever drowned himself in sweat.

Vicious cattle, swollen rivers, and hostile Indians were not the only dangers the new cowboys faced. All too typical was the drive when rancher George Gilland took 1,500 steers from Dallas, Texas, to Dodge City, Kansas. Midway, terrific thunder and lightning stampeded the herd. Balls of fire played around the horns of the steers, the grass was set ablaze, and the air smelled like sulfur. The trail crew could not turn nor stop the stampeding cattle, and they scattered for miles.

Next morning the rancher and a black cowboy, Hamm Harris, tracked some of the herd down a lane to a closed corral. Inside the fence were the steers, and lined along the fence were a dozen armed men.

"Are these your cattle?" one man asked.

"They are," Gilland said.

"They trampled my cornfield," the farmer said. "It'll cost you $50 if you want them back. That's how much my corn was worth."

Gilland and Harris inspected the corn. They found cattle tracks, but they were old tracks, not the fresh tracks the two men had followed to the corral. It was plain that this was a planned robbery. Gilland refused to pay.

Instead, he and Harris loosened their guns in their holsters and rode straight up to the corral. Harris opened the corral gate and guarded it while the rancher drove out the steers. The dozen farmers threatened, but nobody pulled a gun.

Down the lane a piece, Harris and Gilland looked at one another and heaved sighs of relief. Then they

"One Horse Charlie" (center) rode the range in Nevada in the 1880s. He is seen here with two Indian friends.

cheerfully trailed the cattle back to camp. After all, it was just part of a day's work.

Wherever the chuck wagon stopped for the night was home to the trail cowboy, and the cook—more often than not a black man—was "king." But, black or white, he was usually a cranky king, for his job was not easy. Few cowboys crossed him. They said that "crossing a cook is as risky as braiding a mule's tail." They knew what would happen to any cowboy who mistreated the fellow who boiled the beef and beans, baked the sourdough biscuits and molasses pudding, and brewed the coffee. That cowboy would find his coffee bitter, his beans cold, and his biscuits burned to charcoal.

Most cooks are long forgotten, but at least one is remembered for skills other than with pots and pans. No trail crew that rode with Gordon Davis ever forgot the nights around the campfire when the talented black man tuned up his fiddle and played and sang any song a puncher could name. Davis's musical memory seemed inexhaustible, but he always ended the night's concert with his own favorite, "Buffalo Gals, Can't You Come Out Tonight?"

The trail crews had a favorite story about "Add" Addison, who was a black range boss in New Mexico and often headed a trail crew of Texas cowboys. Addison was respected all up and down the Pecos River, so when widely separated ranchers learned that he was getting married, they wanted to send presents. Prompted by their practical wives, the ranchers unknowingly all sent the same thing. On their wedding day Addison and his bride rode to the freight depot to collect their presents. They found nineteen cookstoves waiting for them.

Texas was not the only beef-raising region. Gradually cattlemen in Colorado, then Wyoming, built up their ranches and stocked their ranges. On those ranges the man who won the reputation as the "best top-hand ever to fork a bronc or doctor a sick cow on the Laramie Plains" was Thornton Biggs. The black puncher worked for one of the finest ranches in the West, the Two Bar Ranch owned by Ora Haley. Reports credited Haley's success in the cattle business to Biggs.

"Ora would never have made the fortune he did without Thornt's help," people said.

Biggs himself made no fortune, but he taught dozens of young cowboys—both black and white—the fine points of their trade. He taught them everything about ranching—from how to ride a range and boss a trail crew to how to sell their beef-on-the-hoof for the best price.

When they weren't on the trail, cowboys found plenty to do on the home ranch—round-ups, branding, breaking the wild mustangs brought in from the plains. "Bronc busting," as it was called, was dangerous business, but many cowboys loved it. All over the West there were black cowboys who were superb busters, but the one best remembered was Bill Williams. He lived near the Dakota ranch of Theodore Roosevelt, who later became president of the United States. Roosevelt often watched Williams work and saw how cool, collected, and fearless he was. Roosevelt admired men like that.

No bronc buster stayed in the business long. He got tired of broken bones from being bucked off a horse's back. But there were always new recruits to ride the broncs, and fresh wild broncs to be ridden. They had a saying in the West then:

> *There's never been a horse*
> *that couldn't be rode,*
> *There's never been a man*
> *that couldn't be throwed.*

The grammar was bad, but the thought was true.

9. The Lawmen

Nobody knows how many men served as peace officers in the Old West, nor how many among them were nonwhite. Records were poorly kept. Those that were kept were often lost in the fires that burned down many a wooden courthouse. We do know that of the 250 Texas state police in 1870, nearly one-half were black men. There were black peace officers in Colorado, in California, in New Mexico, and a large number among the deputy United States marshals in the "Indian country" which was the most violent spot on the frontier.

Indian Territory was the red man's land, and for years the tribes dealt out justice to their own wrongdoers. Yet many people who were not Indian also lived in the territory. They had to look to Judge Parker's court at Fort Smith, Arkansas, for their law.

Among those who came to the territory were criminals from all over the nation who were fleeing the law in their old homes. To the lawbreakers the territory looked like a safe place to do what they wanted, and what they wanted was to live by robbery instead of honest work. They thought the Arkansas court too far away to disturb them. They knew Judge Parker had only 200 deputies to patrol the 74,000 square miles with its 60,000 people. No question about it, the Indian country would be safe as rain water! Or so thought the outlaws.

It was true that the Arkansas court had only 200 men, black and white, to do its work, but they were unusual men. They weren't much to look at, perhaps. Certainly they were no storybook heroes. Their clothes were often dusty and in need of pressing. Out on the trail they couldn't shave or get a haircut as often as they might have liked. Day after day, year after year, they rode the timbered hills and long grass pastures of the Indian country.

According to history, "No other American frontier ever saw leagues of robbers so desperate, and hands so red with blood." Yet only the thin line of deputy marshals stood between outlaw and innocent citizen in this wild land.

"Without these men," said Judge Parker, "I could not hold court a single day."

A powerful quartet of deputy U.S. marshals: Amos
Maytubby, Zeke Miller, Neely Factor, and Bob Fortune.

He issued warrants for the outlaw gangs and
told the deputies, "Bring them in alive—or dead."

The 200 deputies did just that—at least those
who were not themselves killed first did. Sixty-five officers died in the line of duty. The records of the black
officers show that they performed "often with outstand-
ing valor and distinction. While many were former
slaves with virtually no educational background, they
successfully carried on the functions of office and had
little attention paid to color." One powerful quartet of
Indian Territory deputies was made up of Neely Factor
and Bob L. Fortune, blacks; Zeke Miller, white; and
Amos Maytubby, Indian. Among other black deputies

whose names are remembered were Grant Johnson, Ed Robinson, Wiley Escoe, Robert Love, Edward Jefferson, Bass Reaves, John Barrett.

On the day John Barrett died, a hot sun seared the prairie. It was July 28, 1895, and most of the citizens in the little town of Okmulgee in Indian Territory were staying indoors to keep cool. But on that day the five-man Rufus Buck gang decided to go on a rampage. Buck was a full-blooded Euchee Indian. The others were of Creek Indian blood. The five men had already earned bad names, and some of them had spent time in the Fort Smith jail. Before their rampage was over they were to be called the "most depraved outlaws in America."

One lone man threatened their plans—John Barrett, a brave and able deputy United States marshal. The Okmulgee area was his district, and he was watching the gang. To the five outlaws, it looked easier to kill him than to dodge him.

So on that summer morning, when the townspeople moved drowsily in the record heat, the Buck gang waylaid the deputy. A half dozen shots rang out. Rufus Buck would later brag that his had been the fatal bullet.

Now, free of any watchful lawman, the gang rode on. Before the day was over the killers had committed four more brutal crimes.

That was only the beginning. For the next thirteen days they rode through the Indian country like a pestilence. Their crimes were cruel and senseless; anybody they chanced to meet was apt to become a victim.

The call to deputies went out from Fort Smith: "Bring them in alive—or dead."

Lawmen gathered for the manhunt and rode out alone, in pairs, in groups. They scoured the plains and dry creek bottoms. They visited lonely farms and ranches, Indian tepees, and rough prairie towns. Behind them rattled the "wagon of the law"—a sort of rolling prison —in which to transport the prisoners after they were captured.

It was hazardous work, and Rufus Buck's cutthroats had the advantage. They could force people to help them and silence them with threats of revenge. They could pay small-time crooks to spy on the deputies' whereabouts.

Even the tracks left by the officers' horses helped the gang. In those days almost all horses in the territory were "barefooted" except ones ridden by lawmen. A track showing that a shod horse had passed by was as good as a sign saying a deputy was near.

The outlaws left signs too. One sign, painted on a board nailed to a big tree, said: "Mr. U.S. Deputy Marshal, this is the dead line. When you cross this line you take your LIFE IN YOUR OWN HANDS."

U.S. Deputy Marshal Bass Reaves was one of the brave lawmen who rode after the Rufus Buck gang.

The deputies read and rode across the line. But they knew they dared not risk a careless moment. They ate with their rifles across their knees. They slept with "one eye open" and a guard posted. The lawmen were tense and exhausted.

Rufus Buck and his gang, on the other hand, were a self-assured and brazen bunch. Dressed in wide-brimmed hats, jeans, and high-topped boots, with vests thrown open and gay bandannas around their necks, they looked like happy cowboys on a spree. Soon like many another criminal, Rufus Buck grew overconfident. On the thirteenth day of terror for the Indian country, the gang held up two stores near the village of McDermott. For the outlaws this was a petty crime, and they took it lightly. To amuse themselves and liven up the "party," they shot at the heels of their victims to make them "dance."

Later, back in their camp a few miles to the south, the five squatted under a tree to divide their loot of tobacco, clothing, and ammunition. That was such an interesting business they did not notice the approach of a posse. The officers opened fire.

Now the outlaws realized their danger. Their horses were picketed too far away to reach. Somehow the five scrambled up a grassy knoll nearby and began to fire on the posse below.

Soon Indian police and angry citizens joined the deputies in the gun battle. The outlaws had picked a good spot from which to fight. The tall grass atop the knoll all but hid them from their attackers. They held their position for seven hours while day turned to dusk and the horses they could not reach calmly switched flies and nibbled at dried prairie grass.

The deputies surrounded the base of the little hill, and time after time they tried to climb it. Each time the outlaws, shooting down from their vantage point, drove the lawmen back.

As the day wore on, word spread through the territory that a posse had found the Buck gang and a battle was in progress. People gathered in the streets of little towns asking one another if the good news could be true. Women and children who had been afraid to step out-of-doors grew suddenly bold. A message even reached faraway Fort Smith, and a bailiff whispered it to Judge Parker, who was holding court. The judge, usually so dignified on the bench, permitted himself a smile.

"Deputy marshals and Indians are engaged in a *hand to hand* conflict with the Buck gang," read the second dispatch to Fort Smith. That message was a bit premature. There was no hand-to-hand grappling until the very end, when the gang, out of ammunition, tried to make a run for freedom, and the deputies swarmed upon them. Amazingly, no one had been killed. But in the final minutes a bullet clipped Rufus Buck's belt, and his sagging trousers added to his troubles.

In chains and under heavy guard, the gang was taken to the railroad town of Muskogee and placed on a train bound for Fort Smith. Then the weary deputies who stayed behind in Muskogee had time for a brief visit home, a change of clothes, and a haircut before they went out again to ride the endless trails.

The rest of the Rufus Buck story moved swiftly. The gang's trial before Judge Parker was short. The five men were found guilty. They appealed their case to a higher court and lost. They were hanged.

Back in the territory, other outlaws spoke bitterly of Judge Parker. "Hanging Parker," they called him, and "Bloody Parker" and "Butcher Parker." But law-abiding citizens called the judge their "Rock of Security," and the deputy marshals gave themselves a new title. They were, they said proudly, the "Men Who Ride for Parker."

Why did they ride? The pay was modest, the glory scant. It was a hard, tense life, and no man knew if he would be alive to see the next sunrise or lying dead from a bullet. Why so many stayed with the life is a source of wonder now. But stay they did, sometimes for many years, riding the trails of the "Old I.T." as the Indian Territory was called by the people who lived there.

They were, indeed, unusual men—iron men. And they, like their brother officers who rode other frontiers from the Mississippi to the ocean's edge, helped make it possible for law-abiding people to settle and develop the West.

10.   The Scouts

The menu for supper was rattlesnake.

There was nothing else—just rattlesnake steak roasted over a greasewood campfire.

It wasn't the sort of meal the army scouts liked best, but it was one they were used to eating. On sandy stretches of border between New and Old Mexico, big rattlers were sometimes the only "game" to be hunted when rations ran out.

Rations had run out now. For two months the Seminole Negro Indian Scouts had trailed Mescalero Apache raiders across the New Mexican desert. They'd lived on half-rations the last week. Now it was rattlesnake for everybody.

The scouts pulled their belts a notch tighter and joked about the snake. Their morale, as usual, was high.

That remarkable morale may be the reason why they were one of the hardest-hitting and most decorated military units ever put in the field by the United States.

When the long strips of roasting "steak" were ready to be eaten, two dozen scouts gathered around the campfire. Pvt. Adam Paine carefully divided the meat into equal portions, and the scouts tackled their meal with more than usual energy, for it took more than usual energy to chew the tough gray snake meat. Supper over, they posted their guard, and the rest of the two dozen scouts rolled up in their blankets and slept under the desert moon.

There were seldom more than two or three dozen men, and never more than fifty in the Seminole Negro Indian Scouts. At times the scouts were attached to an infantry or cavalry unit, black or white. Other times they worked alone, and that was better because few soldiers could keep up with them.

The scouts had one job, and that was to stop Comanches and Apaches from murdering settlers, stealing livestock, and burning homes. Often the Indians struck suddenly, and after a devastating series of raids they would disappear. Far away, in some well-hidden spot, they would rest and wait to strike again. The scouts, quick to follow the trail of the raiders, moved fast, and their skill in tracking was almost unbelievable. On a trail for months at a time, living off the country, they would cross hundreds of miles of mountains and desert to find the hiding place. Then in a surprise attack they would surround and overwhelm the hostile camp just when the Indians were feeling most secure.

No trail was too dim for the scouts. In the Big Bend country of Texas, they once picked up a trail 23 days old and followed it to a mile-high mountain. They left their horses and trudged over the mountain, found the hostiles, killed several including the chief, and recaptured 30 stolen horses and mules.

On such long marches, the scouts could eat snake if they must, but there was no substitute for water. Once, when they were chasing Mescaleros across the sands, their canteens were empty. Thirst can be a fast killer in the desert. The scouts' throats and tongues grew so swollen they could not swallow. Around them their suffering horses staggered, fell, and died.

Then Sgt. David Bowlegs proved his uncanny desert skill. He found a "sleeping spring" that hostile Indians had stopped up and hidden. Using the greatest care, Bowlegs made it flow freely again. Revived by the water, the scouts returned to the chase.

On that trail they were out for 80 days and traveled 1,266 miles. As usual, they found the Indians.

Few regular army troops could perform such feats of endurance and outdoor craft. Few had the scouts' kind of training. They would not have wanted it, because that training was paid for with the pain and blood of runaway slaves.

Most of the scouts were descendants of runaways. Years before the Civil War, their people had fled southern masters and taken refuge among the Seminole Indians of Florida. The fugitives believed that at last they had found a safe and happy life. It was not to be.

Slave catchers came after them. United States military forces were sent to capture or kill them. In order to escape the white men and survive, the runaways had to learn every trick of tracking, enduring hardship, hiding, fighting—how to move silently as smoke, how to vanish in a swamp, how to live on wild plants and the bark of trees.

The children must learn, and the grandchildren too, for even the young would be enslaved if they were caught. It made no difference how many years might have passed. A runaway slave was still a slave, and his children with him.

Then the government moved the reluctant Seminoles from Florida to land that is now Oklahoma. The "black Indians" went with them and found that there was even less safety in the West than in Florida. A slave catcher could be waiting along any trail.

They would go to Mexico, the fugitives decided. That was the only place their families would be safe.

When they reached Mexico the men found that in exchange for places to live they must guard the turbulent Mexican-American border. They had traded one fight for another. But they sharpened their skills in tracking, and they learned to survive the hardships of the desert as they had once learned to survive those of the Florida swamps.

A dozen years later the Civil War made free men of the runaways. Then the United States Army discovered that it badly needed the refugees it had pursued so long and hard. Comanches and Apaches, Lipans and Kickapoos were killing more and more white settlers. They must be found and stopped. Who would know more about hunting the red men than men who had themselves been hunted?

"Bring your horses and join the army as scouts," that was the invitation the government sent the freed men. The men were promised that for their services they would be given $13 a month, shelter and food for their families, and grants of land.

Back across the border came the "black Indians." To men so long homeless, the prospect of land of their own was wonderful.

The Seminole Negro Indian Scouts became a part of the army, with their families living in "Seminole camps" on military reservations in Texas. Under a young white commander, Lt. John Bullis, the scouts began

Seminole Negro Indian Scouts were known as "hard riders, dead shots, and fierce hand-to-hand fighters."

nine years—from 1873 to 1882—of border service and hard-fought combat. Although the enemy sometimes outnumbered them six or eight to one, they never lost a man in battle or had one badly wounded. They did almost lose Bullis, though.

That was on a bright spring day in 1875. The red-faced, black-mustached little lieutenant and three scouts were hunting 75 stolen horses. On the banks of the Pecos River in West Texas, they found the horses and with them 30 Comanche Indians armed with Winchester rifles.

Bullis, Sgt. John Ward, and Privates Isaac Payne and Pompey Factor tethered their mounts and crept to within seventy-five yards of the Comanches. The Indians were too busy trying to get the horses across the river to notice their visitors. The scouts opened fire and kept it up until they had killed three warriors, wounded a fourth, and separated the Indians from their herd. Then the Comanches discovered how few their attackers were.

Scornful of such a puny force, the Indians worked around the little party to cut them off from their horses. The scouts had to run for it.

The scouts reached their mounts and were getting away when Sergeant Ward glanced back. What he saw made his breath catch. Bullis's horse, wild and poorly trained, had broken loose! Bullis was left on foot with Comanches closing in on him and yelling their triumph at the capture.

They yelled too soon, for Sergeant Ward began yelling too: "We can't leave the lieutenant, boys."

Wheeling his horse, the sergeant raced back, closely followed by his two comrades. The Comanches opened a terrific fire, aimed especially at Ward. One bullet cut his gun sling. Another shattered the wooden stock of his gun. That left him without a weapon. But Payne and Factor fought off the swarming Indians while Ward pulled the lieutenant up behind him on his own horse.

"They saved my hair," Bullis said later. Ward, Payne, and Factor each received the Congressional Medal of Honor for their heroism.

The scouts believed their lives were spared in battle because people back home were praying for them.

"When you are fighting for the right and have your trust in God, He will spread His hand over you," they said.

That is how matters stood with the scouts on the desert night when they ate rattlesnake and joked about it. But in the days and months that followed, even the high-spirited scouts found it difficult to laugh. Back in Texas their people were suffering.

The government had shifted the Seminole camp from one military reservation to another, usually because of Texan hostility to the black Indians. Now rations were greatly reduced or, for those who were not regularly enlisted scouts, were cut off entirely. The women tried to find work, but there was little to be had. Old men and boys raised what scant crops they could.

Sometimes the hungry people foraged for stray cattle for food. If they found any, Texans in the area called them thieves.

The greatest blow of all for the scouts was the refusal of the government to make the promised land grants. It was that promise that had brought the 200 men, women, and children to Texas.

To add to the scouts' troubles with the government and Texas citizens, a gang of outlaws known as the "King" Fisher band had a grudge against them. The band viciously murdered two of the scouts and ambushed their old chief, John Horse. He barely escaped with his life.

Then on New Year's Eve in 1877, a Texas sheriff went to the Seminole camp to arrest Adam Paine because of a fight with a black soldier. Instead of making the arrest, the sheriff shotgunned Paine from behind and killed him. The gun blast was so close that Paine's clothing caught fire. Paine had won a Congressional Medal of Honor for heroism in a battle with Cheyenne Indians.

This violence against one of their heroes was the final outrage to the scouts. Some of them left the service and took their families back to Mexico. Yet most of them stayed on, believing that in the end they would receive justice. Lieutenant Bullis did his best to help the men get their land grants. He even enlisted the aid of several army generals. But no grants were ever made to these brave men.

Slowly the Indian raids on the border were coming to a stop. On an April day in 1881, the scouts fought what proved to be their last battle against the Indians.

A small band of Lipans had killed a woman and

a boy in West Texas. Two weeks later the scouts were ordered to go after the raiders.

"You'll not find those Indians," an old-timer told the scouts. "They killed a horse and made shoes for their ponies out of the rawhide so you'll find no tracks."

Rawhide shoes and a trail two weeks old made no difference. The scouts picked up the trail. Over the high rugged mountains and canyons of the Devil's River country it led them, then across the muddy Rio Grande and deep into Mexico. Unlike regular army troops, the scouts could cross the border. In early May they discovered the hostile camp, surrounded it, and made a dawn attack.

Only the raider chief escaped, and he was mortally wounded.

In the sunrise of that May day in Mexico, the scouts finished the job they had left Mexico to do. In the next year, although they covered 3,662 miles of wild southwestern country, they could not find a trace of a single Indian raider.

Now that the Indians were quiet, the army decided it no longer needed its scouts. They were disbanded, and their families put off the military reservations. The land grant promise was forgotten.

The Seminole Negro Indian Scouts did not stop hostile Indian raiding alone, of course. Many brave regular troops of the army fought long and hard too. But history records that:

> without the scouts the work of the regular troops would to a large degree have been futile. The scouts alone could follow a weeks-old trail . . . and terrorize [the Indians] by a surprise attack. . . . Indian campaigns along the border would otherwise have been a series of games of hide-and-seek on a large scale, in which the hostiles, except by rare accident, probably would have been the winners.

> It was to the trailing skill, the endurance, the desert craft of those hard riders, dead shots, and fierce hand-to-hand fighters, the Seminole Scouts, that Texas in a large measure owed her final exemption from such Indian raids as had plagued her borders from her earliest history.

When the scouts were disbanded, some of them remained in the Southwest to eke out a living as best they might.

Others, hopeless of ever winning acceptance from their countrymen, went back to Mexico. As they washed the dust of Texas from their horses' hoofs in the waters of the Rio Grande, they were disappointed men.

But they had kept their part of the bargain with the United States. They had given their country glorious service. They had been paid with inglorious treatment.

All the honor was on their side.

The Old West is gone now. Gone are the buffalo, the Indian tepees, and the hard-riding, gallant-hearted "men in the saddle." It was a time and place of high adventure, and the wonderful stories about how the West was won still live on. Many of the stories are about the stirring deeds of black men, those pioneers who played such an important part in developing the new land. As lawmen, cowboys, scouts, and soldiers they worked and died to make that land their own.

The lure of the unknown and the promise of equal rights drove black men west, but not all of them received the fair treatment they hoped for. Still, no longer slaves, they took their place as free Americans on the western plains where a man was judged by the work he did and not by the color of his skin. Given the chance that had so long been denied, black Americans proved beyond a doubt that they were equal to the challenge of the frontier.